Mabel's Place

by Keesha White
illustrated by Nancy Cote

HOUGHTON MIFFLIN   BOSTON

Printed in China

ISBN 10: 0-618-88630-3
ISBN 13: 978-0-618-88630-2

18 19 20 21 1648 21 20 19 18
4500745690
1118/CA21801280

Mabel sells lemonade.
She has tables in the shade.

2   How many chairs are at each table?

Mice love her tiny tables.
They love to be at Mabel's.

Are the number of mice and chairs the same?   3

One of the mice asks for ice.
Mabel gives ice to all the mice.

4   Which table has more mice?

Mabel fills each paper cup.
The little mice all drink it up.

Which table has fewer mice?   5

The mice ask for cheese.
She asks them to say please.

Does Mabel have more cheese or crackers ?

The little mice thank Mabel.
Mabel thanks them, too.

Are fewer mice staying or leaving?

Mabel's Tables

Draw
Draw 2 tables.

Tell About Monitor Clarify
Tell if Mabel had more chairs or more tables.

Write
Write the words *more*, *fewer* and *all*.